Encantado

Pink Dolphin of the Amazon

Encantado

Pink Dolphin of the Amazon

Sy Montgomery

With photographs by Dianne Taylor-Snow

HOUGHTON MIFFLIN COMPANY • BOSTON 2002

To Thelma or Louise

For information about permission to reproduce selections from
this book, write to Permissions, Houghton Mifflin Company,
215 Park Avenue South, New York, New York 10003.

www.houghtonmifflinbooks.com

Book design by Lisa Diercks
The text of this book is set in Centaur.

Library of Congress Cataloging-in-Publication Data

Montgomery, Sy.
Encantado : pink dolphin of the Amazon / by Sy Montgomery ; photographs by Dianne Taylor-Snow.
p.   cm.
Summary: Introduces the world of the freshwater dolphins called Encantados, or Enchanted, by the people who live near them in the
region of the Amazon and Orinoco rivers in South America.
ISBN 0-618-13103-5
1. *Inia geoffrensis*—Amazon River Region—Juvenile literature. [1. River dolphins. 2. Dolphins. 3. Amazon River Region. 4. Orinoco
River Region (Venezuela and Colombia)] I. Taylor-Snow, Dianne, ill. II. Title.
QL737.C436 M65 2002
599.53'8—dc21
2001039251

Printed in Singapore
TWP 10 9 8 7 6 5 4 3 2 1

Encounters with Encantados

You're traveling to a world that is full of water.

In the Amazon, the wet season lasts half the year. During the rainiest part of the wet season, from March through May, it rains every day. Not all day but every day. Sometimes the rain lasts less than an hour, and then the bright, hot sun comes out to burn your skin. But every day there is some kind of downpour.

The wet season is the best time of year to explore the Amazon. You'll soon see why. So bring a poncho. On your expedition, you will watch the rain remake this jungle world. Swollen with rainwater, the Amazon River and its many branches—smaller rivers called tributaries—

overflow their dry-season banks. The rivers flood people's gardens. Water covers the village soccer fields. The school playgrounds are underwater. Instead of taking a school bus to class, the kids take a canoe.

The village school is like a treehouse, perched high on stilts. Many of the village houses are built on stilts, too. Others float on the river, like rafts. People have to tie their floating houses to big trees so they don't drift away.

On your trip into the Amazon, you'll visit one of these houses. Beneath the floor, you'll hear fishes speaking to one another in clicks and squeaks. At night you'll hear the strange trills of jungle frogs and the voices of birds who stay up all night—and they'll keep you up, too! Some have voices like bells or squeaky chairs; some sound like water falling into a tin cup; some, like tiny flutes or whistles. Some seem to cry out human words. One bird calls, "Too WHY you! Too WHY you!" Another says, with every word getting slower and slower, as if the bird is falling asleep: "Ay . . . yai . . . ma . . . ma."

On your expedition, you'll sleep in a jungle lodge on stilts. You'll visit Amazon villages where the little girls play with real baby caimans (a kind of crocodile) the way girls at home play with dolls—and where the people will tell you stories about amazing creatures they call "encantados."

Encantado means the same thing in Portuguese (the language most people speak in Brazil) and in Spanish (which people speak in Peru and many other South American countries). It means "enchanted." And once you meet an encantado on the river, you'll know why.

You'll never forget your first encounter. Perhaps it will be at the end of the day, when the sunset seems to glow pink on the surface of the water. This is a good time to stop paddling your canoe. Wait for a moment. Watch and listen.

Look at the water beside you. It may seem as if the sunset is glowing a

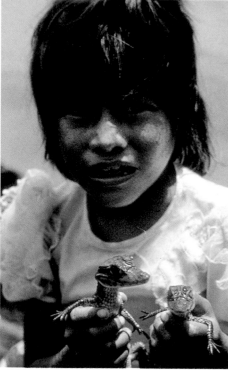

deeper pink on the river. But no—this is no reflection. A creature is swimming up from the depths—an animal nearly as long as the canoe. It's shaped like a dolphin—but it's entirely the wrong color.

It's as pink as a flamingo!

Then, right next to your canoe, a sleek pink face breaks the surface. It's a face that looks like something from an enchanted world—yet it also looks familiar. Long, tube-shaped lips stick out like a nose. The forehead is rounded and as big as a melon. The creature's pearl-gray eyes look right into yours. It opens a hole in the top of its head and gasps.

"CHAAAHHH!"

And then it dives back out of sight.

Who are these strange creatures?

That's what you've come to the Amazon to find out.

9

THE ENCANTADOS GO BY MANY NAMES.

Scientists call them by their species name, *Inia geoffrensis* (IN-ee-yuh Jeff-REN-sis). That's the Latin name for the pink dolphin. It lives only in the Amazon and in one other South American river, the Orinoco (OAR-in-OH-ko). And although they're about the same size as some of the dolphins you've seen performing in aquariums and zoos—they grow more than six feet long and may weigh 400 pounds—they are very different from oceangoing dolphins. And not only because of their color.

You're about to meet one of the most mysterious dolphins in the world. Scientists are eager to find out more about them. They could use your help. But studying them can be extremely difficult—as you'll soon find out.

In Brazil the encantados are also called by a local word, *boto* (BO-toe). When your Brazilian friends find out you're studying the pink dolphins, they'll probably give you this advice: "Cuidado como boto!" (Kwee-DAH-doe comb-oh-BO-toe.) In Brazilian Portuguese, that means, "Be careful with those pink dolphins!"

Why do you need to be careful? People here believe the pink dolphins are enchanted and have magical powers—including the power to steal you away to a magical world beneath the river. It's a world so beautiful, they say, that once you visit, you will never want to leave.

In Peru people believe the dolphins are magical too. As well as encantado, another name people call the pink dolphin is *bufeo colorado* (Boo-FEY-oh co-low-RAH-doe). *Bufeo* is the local word for dolphin, and *colorado* is Spanish for ruddy or reddish. Some of these dolphins are so rosy they are almost red; some are pink as flamingos. Others are paler pink, like bubblegum.

And some of the "pink" dolphins are really not pink at all. Some are light gray, some are dark gray. And some look gray one minute and turn pink the next—like a person who is blushing. No wonder people think these creatures are enchanted.

Beneath the river, the people say, is a world so beautiful you would never want to leave it.

This also makes the pink dolphins difficult to study. It's hard to keep track of a creature who changes color from minute to minute—*and* spends most of its life beneath the water, where you can't even see it.

But don't give up. When you begin your travels with pink dolphins, you might find yourself doing things you thought were impossible:

You'll canoe through the treetops.

You'll explore an underwater jungle.

You'll even take a trip back through time.

And you never know what important discoveries you might make along the way.

One thing's for certain: if you follow the pink dolphins into the Amazon, they will lead you to an amazing world—a world full of surprises and mysteries—and perhaps even some magic.

Whales of the Amazon

Everything about them sounds impossible: pink dolphins! Dolphins who live in rivers, not in the ocean. And not just any rivers: these are rain-forest dolphins, who swim in a submerged jungle.

And look how they do it. Unlike the athletic dolphins who jump through hoops for aquarium shows, pink dolphins don't leap out of the water. Watch: they swim slowly, low in the water. They don't look like "regular" dolphins, either: Unlike the ones who swim in the sea, the pink dolphin doesn't have a tall, pointed fin on the back, sticking out of the water like a shark's. Pink dolphins just have a low ridge, which makes them difficult to spot.

All Dolphins Are Whales,
and Some Whales Are Dolphins

Wʜᴀᴛ sᴏʀᴛ ᴏꜰ ᴄʀᴇᴀᴛᴜʀᴇs ᴀʀᴇ ᴛʜᴇsᴇ ᴘɪɴᴋ ᴅᴏʟᴘʜɪɴs, ᴀɴʏᴡᴀʏ?

Long ago, people thought dolphins and whales were fish. After all, they have fins like fish and live in the water. But no—whales and dolphins are mammals. Like dogs and cats, monkeys and elephants, pandas and people, they are warm-blooded, they feed their babies with milk, and they breathe air. (That's what the hole at the top of the head is for—the blowhole is really the nostrils.)

But dolphins and whales are special kinds of mammals. They all have the same basic torpedolike shape. They live in the water their whole lives (unlike seals, for instance, who come out of the water onto land to mate and have babies.) They are called cetaceans (see-TAY-shuns). This name comes from the Latin word *cetus*, which means whale. So all dolphins are really different kinds of whales.

When people say "dolphin," they're usually thinking of one particular species: the bottlenosed dolphin. These are the dolphins you see performing in aquariums and zoos. But there are lots of other kinds, too. Almost all of them live in oceans, not rivers.

The marine dolphins are real athletes. They're acrobats, too. One kind, the spinner dolphin, twists and spins in midair when it leaps out of the water. Marine dolphins are built for speed swimming in the open ocean. The tall fin on the back helps them slice through the water. Scientists include the black and white killer whale or orca with the marine dolphins.

The pink dolphin, though, comes from a very different branch of the whale family. Only five kinds of whales have bodies modified to live in fresh water. All of them look very different from the marine dolphins. All have a long narrow snout and a low fin on the back. One of them, the baiji, lives in the great Yangtze River of China. Because this river is about to be interrupted by a huge dam, most scientists think the baiji will be extinct in only a few years. Fewer than thirty survive today. Another kind of river dolphin, the Gangetic dolphin, lives in the Ganges river system of India and Bangladesh. The Indus River dolphin lives in the rivers of Pakistan, near India. In South America, the La Plata dolphin lives in the river of that name, south of the Amazon. And finally, there's our encantado, the pink dolphin of the Amazon.

Sometimes it even seems the pink dolphin is playing hide-and-seek with you. One might be right next to your canoe and you won't know it—until it surprises you: "CHAAAH!" And then dives again.

Beneath the water—maybe even right beneath your canoe—pink dolphins are doing things that no oceangoing dolphin could possibly do. Some of the Amazon's many rivers are clear and blue, but most of them are not. Some are cloudy, full of little particles of rock, like dust in the water. Some are stained dark as night with the natural chemicals from rain-forest leaves. The pink dolphin can navigate them all—even inky waters jammed with underwater branches.

How do they do it? All dolphins can see quite well, both in and out of water. But they also have a secret sense that we humans don't. It works almost like Superman's X-ray vision, but with a twist: they can "see" with sound.

It seems impossible. You can't even see ears on a dolphin or a whale. That's because their ears are hidden, like so many other things about their lives.

The ears are inside the body, in back of the lower jawbone. And their hearing is excellent.

With ears you can't see, dolphins chart their world with echoes from sounds you can't hear—but dolphins can.

Besides making sounds from their mouths, dolphins (as well as many whales) can also send out pulses of sound, like an invisible beam of light, from inside their foreheads. The sound beams are too high-pitched for our ears. Listening with the help of special underwater microphones and recording devices, scientists have learned that these sounds are a series of pulsed

clicks. The clicks travel through the water. When they hit an object—a tree branch, a tasty fish, or even a swimming person—the sounds come bouncing back to the dolphin. That's right—it's an echo. Dolphins can locate objects by their echoes. That's why this sense is called echolocation. It's also sometimes called sonar, which ships and submarines use to probe the water, too.

In fact, the echoes form a three-dimensional image in the dolphin's brain, allowing the animal to "see" not only the object's shape and size but also its insides. Doctors use this sort of sonar to see inside people's bodies. A doctor may have used ultrasonography to see you inside your mother's body before you were born.

For millions of years, before sailors had submarines with sonar or doctors could make sonograms, dolphins have been probing their

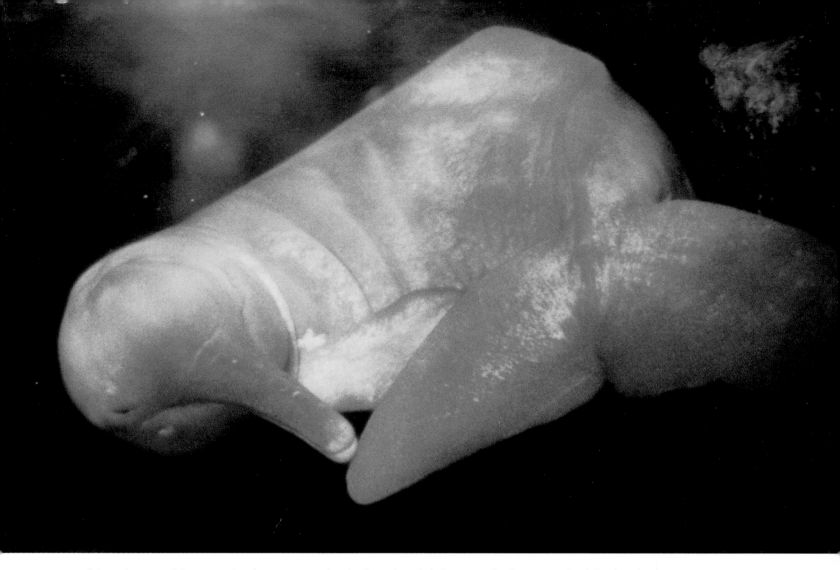

world with sound beams. And scientists think that the dolphins with the most highly developed sense of echolocation are the pink dolphins of the Amazon. They need it to navigate the underwater obstacle course of the flooded forest.

In addition to this super-sonar, pink dolphins have another special talent. Ocean dolphins' bodies don't bend very well. They'd never be able to get around all the branches in the Amazon. Pink dolphins can bend their bodies to twist gracefully through the underwater treetops. They are so flexible they can even touch their tail to their nose—like a dolphin doughnut.

Because of their unique flexibility, pink dolphins can also swim in shallow waters that ocean dolphins can't manage. Sometimes they get stuck—but not for long. You probably have already noticed that pink dolphins have really big front flippers—almost like wings. At moments like these, those flippers come in handy. Pink dolphins can use their front flippers not just to swim but also to crawl—both out of and back into the water!

Sometimes pink dolphins' behavior seems downright weird. Here's another example: sometimes they sleep upside down. Imagine finding a 300-pound dolphin floating upside down like a dead goldfish! Why do they do this? Why don't other dolphins?

No one knows. And that's just one of the mysteries about them.

Pink dolphins really don't seem much like dolphins at all. And no wonder. They are very different animals from the dolphins you've seen frolicking in the ocean and starring on TV. So different, in fact, that some scientists tell us it might be best to think of the Amazon's pink dolphins as ancient river-living whales.

These pink dolphins—or river whales—are designed for an entirely different kind of life than oceangoing dolphins. You can see that in the way they swim and the way they're shaped. But when you think about it, everything about their unusual behavior and undolphinlike bodies makes perfect sense.

No wonder pink dolphins don't leap out of the water—they often swim in the shallows. No wonder they don't have that tall fin on the back—they'd be constantly bumping it on underwater branches. Ouch! And even though they don't swim as far or as fast as oceangoing dolphins, the pink dolphins can go where no marine dolphin has gone before: into inky black shallows, and even (briefly) onto land.

You may have heard stories about marine dolphins saving people from drowning at sea or guiding fishing boats to big schools of fish. They've even helped lost sailors find shore.

The pink dolphins can do something more. Of all the dolphins in the world, they alone —with their super-sonar, winglike flippers, and graceful, bending bodies—can help you explore the hidden, watery mysteries of the Amazon's jungle rivers.

So congratulations! You've picked the perfect guide to lead you into the Amazon—a world so big, so strange, and so full of life that it feels like it's enchanted.

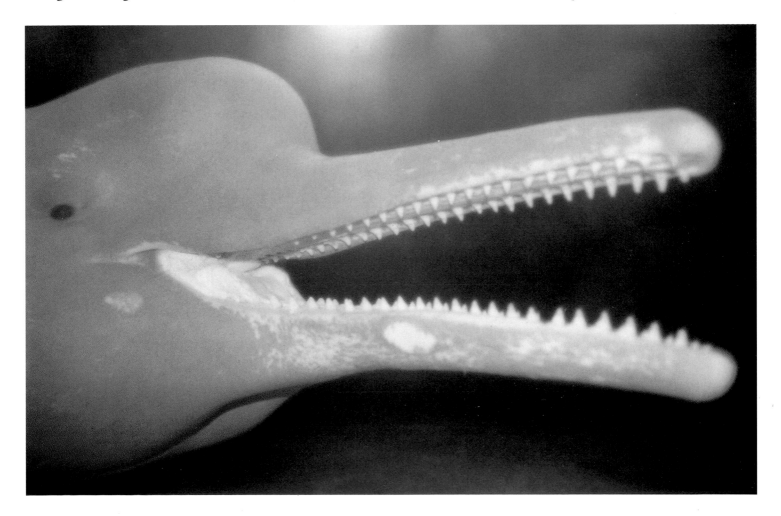

Nightmare Dream World

CANOEING THROUGH THE FLOODED FOREST FEELS LIKE A DREAM.

Around you, treetops poke out of the water at eye level. You don't have to look up to see the beautiful orchids that flower on tree branches: they are right in front of you. As you canoe through the treetops, you can see the tree hollows where parrots nest. You can look straight into the hole where a mother bamboo rat is raising her babies. You might even find yourself face to face with a three-toed sloth.

A bamboo rat.

Strange lives cling to every tree. Fist-sized, hairy megalomorph spiders, who look like tarantulas, hunt for bugs in tree holes. The purselike nests of little birds called oropendulas hang from the tips of branches. Centipedes curl in the cracks of bark. Snails cling to the undersides of leaves.

"Duck!" Moises Chavez (MOY-sess SHAH-vez), your Peruvian guide, calls out from the front of the boat.

A duck? Where? But no—he motions you to get your head down, fast. You don't want to smack your head on a low branch as the canoe glides beneath it. Particularly this branch—because hanging down from it is a wasp nest the size of a pumpkin.

Fortunately, Moises knows these waterways well. He can warn you of the dangers. He grew up in the Amazon rain forest. His father was a teacher working in Amazonian Indian villages. Moises speaks some of the Indian languages, as well as Spanish and English. He has learned many of the jungle's secrets, including where to find the pink dolphins.

Today he's taking you to his favorite lake, where he knows you'll see pink dolphins. But to get there, you have to thread through twisting waterways, the heart of the Amazon rain forest.

ABOVE: *No one is likely to disturb these two families of oropendula birds, which have wisely woven their grass nests next to a nest of stinging wasps.* BELOW: *Hairy megalomorph spiders defend themselves with the hairs on their legs.*

Beneath you is an underwater jungle. Swimming through the branches of the swamped trees are fish with eyes like jewels and fish with teeth like daggers. Some of the creatures who live here are so strange they seem like something out of a science fiction thriller: turtles who use tiny pieces of flesh on their tongues to lure fish right into their mouths. Electric eels as long as limousines. Packs of hungry piranhas. Not to mention dolphins who are bright pink.

SMACK!

Something has hit you on the shoulder. When you turn around, you see nothing. But something silvery is flopping around in the canoe right by your sneakers. It's a four-inch-long dogfish with inch-long, needlelike teeth!

Moises picks up the dogfish carefully by the tip of the tail and flings it back into the water. "This guy was looking for a bug," he explains. In the Amazon's enchanted world, not even the fish behave the way they're supposed to. Some of them hunt by leaping into the air.

Lucky for you it wasn't an arauana. This fish grows to be a yard long. It swims with its chin whiskers pointing forward and its eyes half above the surface, allowing it to see above and below water at the same time. Like the dogfish who jumped into your boat, when it spots something to eat —a beetle, a spider, sometimes a bird or a bat—it leaps out of the water. It can jump as high as six feet to grab its meal right out of a tree. One scientist watched in amazement as an arauana leapt from the water and snatched a baby sloth right out of its mother's arms!

Above you, vines coil into the tops of the trees. The vines

LEFT: *A centipede.* RIGHT: *An electric eel.*

are hungry, too: they are hunting for light, from which they make their own food. Follow the vines up to the sky: you'll see red and gold macaw parrots zoom by, bright blue tail feathers trailing. The sun beats down hard, even though it's early in the morning. Good thing you brought sunscreen and a wide-brimmed hat.

Trees poke out of the water on all sides. Moises explains that it's important to keep your hands away from the sides of the boat. It's easy to see why. Some of the trees have spines growing out of their trunks. "They're sharp as needles," he says. "Don't touch the trees! See this guy"—he points to a tree with smooth bark—"this guy has sap that can burn your skin. And this guy," he says, pointing to a short tree with yellow flowers, "from its leaves you can make a tea to cure yellow fever. And this guy—"

BANG!

Your canoe has come to an abrupt halt. The bottom is hung up on an underwater tree limb.

Your canoe is stuck in the treetops! Bet you didn't think that would be a problem when you left the United States. Though that was only yesterday, it seems a long time ago.

ABOVE: *Moises Chavez at the helm of the canoe.* BELOW: *Some trees protect themselves with sharp spines.*

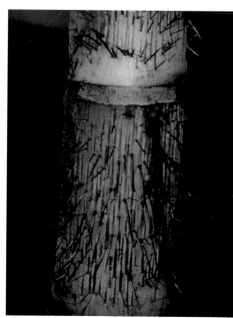

Yesterday probably seems like a blur. You took an airplane from Miami, Florida, to Iquitos, Peru, and landed in another world. Iquitos is the capital of the Peruvian province of Loreto. It's a province the size of Spain, but there are no paved roads into the jungle. To reach the Rainforest Lodge, you spent the rest of the day on a motorized boat on the Amazon River.

On that trip you probably realized for the first time just what a big place the Amazon is.

The Amazon River stretches for 4,000 miles. It holds half the world's river water—fourteen times the flow of North America's mighty Mississippi. Its waters nourish a forest that spreads for 2.5 million square miles—nearly half the size of the moon! On the trip to your jungle lodge, there were times when you couldn't even see the banks of the river. It looked as big as an ocean.

The Amazon jungle is not only a giant land, it's a land of giants: spiders with bellies as big around as tangerines, lily pads as big as throw rugs, giant river otters nine feet long.

But what's most amazing about the Amazon isn't the size of its creatures. It's all the different forms they take. Just think: the Mississippi has about 250 different kinds of fish, and the Congo River in Africa has about a thousand, but the Amazon has more than 2,500 different species of fish.

They come in every shape and size you can imagine—plus quite a few you might not. Consider the shark-sized pirarucu (peer-uh-ROO-koo), whose tongue is covered with teeth. (At least it doesn't have to worry about biting its tongue!) Then there's the electric eel, whose tail has special organs that produce an electric charge to stun its prey like a ray gun. (Sometimes, though, an electric eel won't bother to stun a fish—it can also suck one through its open mouth directly into its stomach, like a vacuum cleaner.)

There are fish in the Amazon who build nests in trees, fish who care for their babies by protecting them inside the father's mouth. There are fish who could eat you—such as the several different kinds of piranhas. Hunting in packs like hyenas, they search out flailing and injured creatures in the water. Together, they tear the flesh from their prey.

At dinner at the lodge that first night, before crawling beneath your mosquito net to sleep, perhaps you sampled some of these fishes for dinner. The lodge often serves red-bellied piranha. It's full of little bones but tastes delicious.

And besides, it's much more fun to eat a piranha than the other way around.

You may be thinking about those hungry piranhas now, or

Moises Chavez grew up in the Amazon and learned its secrets— including how to find this "red water vine," which gives you a cool, clean drink when you're thirsty.

about the big crocodiles of the Amazon, called caimans. Or about poisonous snakes—like the bushmaster, the world's largest pit viper. It grows to fifteen feet and stabs its victims repeatedly with massive, poisonous fangs.

Jaguars. Vampire bats. Anacondas—giant snakes who hug you to death and then swallow you whole. They could be lurking all around you. And there you are, like a sitting duck, stuck in your canoe in a tree in the middle of the jungle!

But Moises quickly gets the situation under control by pushing against a tree to free the canoe.

You're over the log, but you're not out of trouble.

"Watch out!" calls Moises. "Tangarana tree!"

Moises recognizes the tree's long, oval leaves right away. And he also knows that its hollow stems teem with thousands of stinging black tangarana ants. Each ant is more than an inch long. When something bumps against the tree, the ants think it's an attack on their home. Bravely, they'll rush to defend it. They'll even jump off branches into your canoe to sting you if they think their tree is threatened.

ABOVE: *A man holds a bushmaster.*
BELOW LEFT: *A caiman.* BELOW RIGHT: *A piranha.*

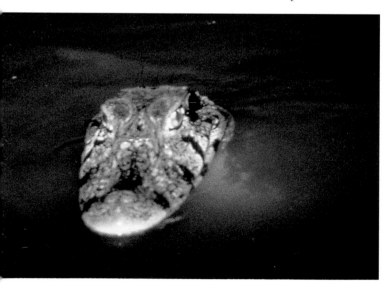

A giant lily pad.

At the last minute, with some skilled paddling, Moises veers the canoe away from its dangerous path. You miss the ant tree by inches.

And then, pushing aside some branches like a curtain on a stage, Moises reveals your destination: the dolphin lake. You've made it.

During the dry season, the lake is little more than a puddle. But now, full of rainwater, it covers an area larger than a thousand football fields. It's shaped like a figure eight, with the crown of a mimosa tree poking up the middle.

Across the lake you can hear a dolphin blowing: "CHHHAAA!"

Reflections on the Water

You're surrounded.

At first, it seemed that you would see the dolphins only far away—just a pink shimmer on the water's surface. At first glance, you weren't sure whether you really saw one or just imagined it.

But Moises had a great idea. "Let's call them," he suggested. He leaned over the side of the canoe and, reaching underwater, banged on the side of the boat with his knuckles. The dolphins responded. And now they are all around you.

Right behind your canoe, you hear one blow. You twirl around, but all you see is the dolphin's wake, the wave it made when it dived just a split second ago. Then— "CHAAHHH!" A dolphin surfaces in front. "Look!" cries Moises—but you see only a trail of bubbles.

SPLASH! Off to your left, a big pink form has surfaced. But by the time you turn, you see only a tail.

It seems as if dolphins are everywhere—and nowhere.

You can hear their breath almost in your ears. You catch a glimpse—and then it disappears. Even though the dolphins are quite close, when you lean over and look into the water, you see nothing. It's as if the dolphins simply vanish into the water, the way a magician disappears in a puff of smoke.

If the water were clear, as in an aquarium tank, you could see them swimming beneath the surface. But the water in the lake is as dark as night. It's not polluted; it's stained with natural chemicals from decaying rain-forest leaves.

Because of the dark water, it's impossible to count the dolphins. It certainly seems there are several. After all, one

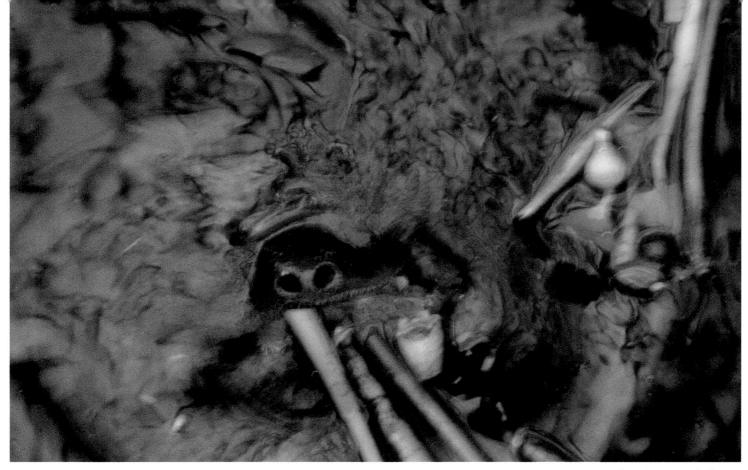

surfaced in back of the boat, then one in front of the boat. Another rose to the side. Does that mean there were three dolphins?

Maybe not. Remember that pink dolphins, with their bendy bodies, don't have to swim in a straight line. You can't predict where they might surface next. They can turn and twist beneath the water, even whirl around like a Ferris wheel. Maybe the three glimpses you had were all of the same dolphin.

How would you tell? Most animals, including dolphins, look as different from one another as people do. You just have to learn to see the differences. Some are bigger than the others, some are darker. One might have a notch or a scar on the back or head. One might have a bent snout.

But here's the problem: because pink dolphins don't leap out of the water, and because the lake water is so dark, you never see much of any individual dolphin at one time. You get only little glimpses: the glistening pink top of a head here, a tail there, a quick look at the low fin on the back here. And you can't identify them by color, because these dolphins grow pinker with exercise, just as people do.

The water is so dark you can't tell who might be swimming in there with you! This nose belongs to a huge Amazonian manatee.

For half an hour, the dolphins, whether one or several, continue to visit near your canoe. Could they be as curious about you as you are about them?

AFTER A HEARTY LUNCH BACK AT THE LODGE — PEANUT BUTTER AND JELLY sandwiches, a salad of tomatoes and cucumbers, and juicy fresh pineapple for dessert—you decide to return to the lake. Will the dolphins still be there?

The water is as still as glass. You watch for an hour, scanning everywhere with your binoculars. Nothing.

But it's a beautiful afternoon. There are plenty of sights to enjoy. The sky is alive with birds. A huge flock of white egrets drifts overhead, like wisps of cloud. A flock of green mealy parrots calls, "OW-ow-ow-ow-ow!" Their cries sound like those of a person who is trying to run over hot coals in bare feet.

Home sweet home: the Rainforest Lodge

Other birds are hidden, but Moises knows where to look. In the thorny crown of a small mimosa, he points out the tiny, cup-shaped nest of a pair of white-banded antbirds. It's only a little bigger than a hummingbird's nest and holds two speckled eggs.

At the end of the day, with your canoe tethered to a tree, you watch the pink glow of the sinking sun reflecting on the water. Pink—like the dolphins. It is as if the sky is calling them. And just at that moment, a pink face breaks the surface.

You're face to face for a look that seems to last both forever and only a second. The pink dolphin's pearl-gray eye looks into yours. Then the creature opens the blowhole at the top of the head. "CHAAAH!" Your face is wet with the dolphin's spray. And then it dives.

That does it—you've fallen under their spell.

As you and Moises paddle back to the lodge for dinner, you're full of questions about the dolphins. How many of them visit the lake? Do they stay there all year, or do they move to

ABOVE: *Egrets may cover a tree like snow.*
LEFT: *White-banded antbirds weave a nest as small as a hummingbird's.*

This pink dolphin looks almost like a reflection on the water.

other lakes and rivers? Are there mothers with babies among them? What kinds of fish do they like to eat?

Moises knows a lot about the wildlife in the Amazon. But even he doesn't know the answers to your questions. "The bufeo, they are very mysterious," he says.

His answer only makes you more curious.

How can you find out more?

STUDYING PINK DOLPHINS IS THRILLING . . . AND FRUSTRATING.

They're so close, and yet most of the time so invisible. How can you study an animal you can't even see?

If only there were some way to see them better.

Have you ever swum in the ocean or a pond with your eyes open or with a diver's mask? You can watch all kinds of fish and crabs that way.

And that gives you an idea: maybe you could see the dolphins better if you were right in the water with them.

Of course, there's the little matter of the piranhas, the electric eels, and the dagger-toothed dogfish . . .

"No problem," says Moises. He likes your idea. Lots of visitors to the lodge swim in this lake. No one has ever been hurt. And besides, with Moises watching you and a life vest to help keep you afloat, you should be perfectly safe.

Books about the Amazon tell you the same thing: piranhas are dangerous to people only at certain places and at certain times of year. In fact, most piranha bites happen on boats, when a person tries to remove a piranha from a fish hook. As for the dogfish and the electric eels, you have nothing to fear. If you don't bother them, they won't bother you.

While you canoe to the lake with Moises, you keep thinking about the moment when you'll jump overboard into night-dark water. You can't help but wonder: maybe those fish haven't read those books!

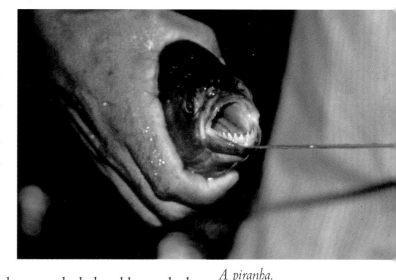

SPLASH! After the long canoe ride in the hot sun, the water feels great. It even helps soothe some of those itchy mosquito bites you've accumulated during the ride. The dark lake water is as smooth as a black satin sheet against your skin. You tread water for a moment, enjoying the cool.

"There!" says Moises. Across the lake, he can see a pink dolphin in the distance.

Now for the moment of truth. Taking a big breath, you sink your whole head beneath the water. You open your eyes.

A piranha.

You can't even see your own feet. The water is just too dark to see anything.

You had a wonderful swim that day. It was both an adventure and an experiment. And sometimes the results of an experiment are disappointing. In the water you tested your idea and got your answer: at least for now, at least in this lake, you can't watch the dolphins underwater.

So you'll have to think of another way that might work. Any ideas?

Maybe you need to look at things from a new angle. When you need to see something better, what do you do? You may rub your eyes. You may try binoculars. Or you may try to find a better position to see.

Wait a minute . . . maybe that's the answer. Perhaps from a great height you could look straight down into the water. Perhaps from the top of a tall tree, you could see the dolphins better.

But how to get up into the tree?

Moises has an idea. At the edge of another lake, a sturdy rope hangs from a big tree. The rope can be hooked up to the sort of harness that climbers use to scale mountains.

There's nothing you won't try—but climbing up into a tree to look for pink whales in the Amazon? Sounds crazy. But the next day, that's exactly what you do.

Leather loops grip the tops of your thighs and your lower belly. There's a noose for one foot. You step into the noose and, as if you were climbing a stair and straightening your leg, you push yourself up, clinging on to the rope with gloved hands.

Progress is slow. Push with the leg. Pull with both arms. Rest. Push, pull, rest. Up and up you climb. Up . . . past a big brown termite nest that smells like cedar. Up . . . past a big philodendron vine with leaves shaped like giant, outstretched hands. Up . . . until you find yourself inside a forest in the tree.

Besides the tree's own leaves, there are ferns growing up here, and flowers, mosses, even a cactus! These plants are epiphytes (EH-pih-fights). What they all have in common is this: they are plants that grow without soil, perching harmlessly on the tree's branches.

As you climb higher, you see the white flower of an orchid. It's so close you can even smell it. Mmmmmm—it smells like vanilla. Now you've made a discovery: the vanilla "bean" that flavors ice cream, cakes, and cookies is actually the seedpod of a tropical orchid. And in the Amazon, there are more than 250 kinds of vanilla orchids alone.

Finally you reach the top of the rope. You've climbed the equivalent of seven stories up this tree. "Hooray!" Moises calls up from the canoe. And now you look down . . . down past butterflies flying below you . . . down past an oropendula bird zooming to its nest in the next tree . . . down at the canoe. Moises looks about two inches tall. And below the canoe is the black water.

It's seven stories to the ground from the top of this machimango tree.

But alas—you still can't see beneath the water's surface. The dolphins' underwater world is still as mysterious as night.

On the climb down, though, you look into another body of water. A plant you hadn't noticed before catches your eye. Like the orchids and cactuses and ferns, it's an epiphyte, perched on a branch. With its spiky leaves, it looks like the top of a pineapple. It's called a bromeliad (bro-MILL-ee-ad). Its overlapping leaves form a bowl as big as a water glass—a bowl that catches rainwater.

As you descend, you take a look inside that bowl. And here you make another discovery. It's a tiny lake, and it's full of life. An inch-long blue and black frog clings to the edge of the minilake with suction-cup fingers. A little brown beetle oars through the water with strong back legs. A yellow and black spider has spun a tiny web across the water, and beneath it swim squiggly larvae, the water-living baby stage of mosquitoes. Little jellylike balls float,

each the size of the head of a pin. They are the eggs of a tree frog who lives its whole life in this small bowl of water high in the tree!

What you've discovered is actually a tiny treetop world unto itself. In fact, scientists have counted more than 500 different species of creatures who can be found living in the minia-ture rainwater-world of a bromeliad's bowl.

THIS IDEA DIDN'T WORK OUT QUITE THE WAY YOU'D PLANNED. YOU WERE TRYING to see beneath the water—but ended up climbing into a plant world in the air. You were look-ing for dolphins from the treetops—and instead found a whole world you never thought existed.

Your mission up the tree didn't fail. Instead, it succeeded in ways you couldn't have imag-ined. But when you're exploring scientific mysteries, you never know what might happen.

Especially when you're following encantados.

Science at the Edge of Your Senses

THIS ISN'T GOING TO BE EASY.

Studying wild animals never is easy. But that doesn't mean you're doing something wrong. Difficult problems are always the most important ones to solve—and the ones with the most surprises.

Vera da Silva has studied pink dolphins longer than any other researcher.

Only a handful of scientists have ever tried to study pink dolphins. One of them is Vera da Silva. A scientist specializing in water-living mammals, Vera has studied pink dolphins longer than any other researcher—more than twenty years. She lives and works in Manaus, Brazil, 2,300 miles down the Amazon from Iquitos. If only there were some way to ask her advice.

You're a long way from a phone or e-mail; there are no electric or telephone lines in the jungle. But there is a shortwave radio at the lodge. Maybe you can reach Vera at her office at the Amazon Research Institute in Manaus, where she runs the Marine Mammal Laboratory.

"Oi!" answers Vera, the Brazilian version of "Hi!" But she soon switches to English when she realizes what you want to know.

"Oh, yes, there is so much still to learn from the botos," she says, her Brazilian accent mixing with static over the radio. "They are so beautiful and so mysterious. You must be very persistent!"

Vera knows all about persistence, about sticking to a goal even when the job seems difficult or even impossible. She has always loved nature. As a child growing up on a farm, she collected insects and frogs. She made a small museum in her house to display her collection. "My sisters used to hate me!" she says. They didn't like to share a room full of bugs and frogs.

When she grew up, Vera went to university to study Amazonian wildlife. Her father, a farmer, didn't understand. "Why study dolphins?" he asked. "You won't make a lot of money that way." But Vera continued her studies. She didn't care if her work never made her rich. She loved the dolphins' beauty and was fascinated by the mysteries about them. And she hoped that her work would one day help people learn how to protect the pink dolphins and the Amazon rain forest. "We have the choice," she says, "to protect it or not."

She knows that animals in the Amazon face grave dangers—often from people who burn the forests to clear the land. They are clearing it not just for little farms, as people have done for thousands of years. Now people are burning land for giant corn plantations and for herds of hundreds of cattle. When the fires burn out of control, they kill everything in their path. And the destruction is so vast, the forest doesn't grow back—ever.

Big companies that mine gold and explore for oil pollute the rivers. They poison the fishes and manatees, dolphins and otters. Huge fleets of fishing ships invade the lakes and rivers. With enormous nets, they catch and kill everything they find—including dolphins. The boats' big propellers hit the slow-moving, gentle manatees. At the Marine Mammal Laboratory, Vera helps care for half a dozen orphaned manatees whose mothers were killed by boat propellers. And with her husband, Robin Best, Vera often raised orphaned animals who were victims of human meddling. Together they raised an orphaned anteater, a baby bush dog, and several sloths. One of the sloths, a female

A fire set to clear land for crops and cattle.

Holding a sloth.

named Pooh, used to live in the office. She would climb up Robin's legs as if he were a tree!

But the work Vera likes best is far from the office. Her favorite thing is studying dolphins in the wild. She especially likes it when her daughters, ages eleven and thirteen, can come along.

Sometimes Vera spends weeks, every day from dawn till dusk, just watching the dolphins. When she sees one, she notes the time on her watch, the weather, and what the dolphin is doing. But some days she can't find them at all. She has cruised thousands of miles of river on big boats looking for dolphins, trying to find out where they live and where they don't. She has spent hundreds of hours in a small canoe like yours, tied to a tree in the same place all day. She has also climbed up big trees to try to watch them swim below her.

And she, too, has found the job of studying pink dolphins frustrating as well as thrilling.

"To be a biologist, you do crazy things," she says. "You have to fix boat engines. You have to climb high into trees just to study the animals. Sometimes you don't get the answers, sometimes you do. And sometimes you get a new answer you didn't expect."

Like all good scientists, Vera has written up her findings. Published in journals, her reports encourage other researchers—like you—to build on her work.

Vera has made some very important discoveries. One of them was finding out what the pink dolphins eat. The answer is: everything!

Every time Vera happens upon a dead dolphin, she cuts open its stomach to see what it was eating. She sorts the fish into categories and records every species. She has found more than fifty different species on the dolphins' menu. Giant catfish and little piranhas. Silvery arauanas and the strange pirarucu with teeth on its tongue. In fact, a pink dolphin might eat more kinds of fish in one meal than other species of whales eat in a lifetime.

Vera also helped find out just where the pink dolphins can be found. By pooling her observations with those of other scientists working in the South American countries of Colom-

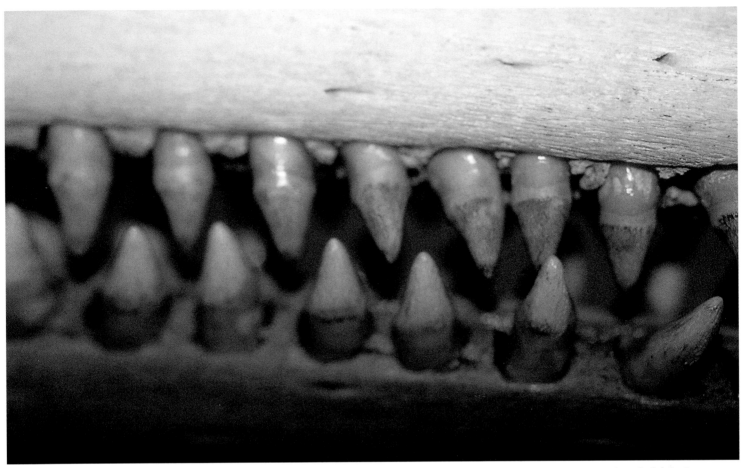

A pink dolphin's jaws bear 130 strong, cone-shaped teeth.

bia, Peru, Bolivia, and Ecuador, she has discovered that pink dolphins are found in most of the major tributaries of both the Amazon and the Orinoco. They can live in flooded forests and deep rivers. They can live in waters as dark as ink—like the Rio Negro. (*Rio* means river in both Spanish and Portuguese; *negro* means black.) They can live in water that's so cloudy with sediment it looks almost like chocolate milk—like the Rio Solimões. They can also live in clear, blue waters—like the lower reaches of the Rio Tapajos.

Vera measures how fast the pink dolphins swim: about nine miles per hour. She measures how often they need to breathe: about once every two minutes. She sorts out the different situations in which she sees dolphins: how many times they are alone, how often in the company of another dolphin, and whether the dolphin companions are many or few, big or little. Most of the time, the pink dolphins she has watched travel alone. The next most common type of sighting she has recorded is of a mother dolphin with her baby. Mothers and babies stay together for at least two and a half years.

The meeting of the waters: in Manaus, Brazil, the milky white water of the Rio Solimões and the darker water of the Rio Negro meet but don't mix. They flow side by side for miles. Pink dolphins can live in both kinds of water—and in clear water, too.

Vera usually watches the dolphins from a canoe. She has the same problem you have: it's hard, if not impossible, to tell who's who when you can see only a little piece of a dolphin at a time. But she keeps going, entranced by the mysteries of the encantados and enchanted by their grace, their curiosity, and the sheer pleasure of their company.

"If you stop your boat for several hours, they will just come over," she says. "You can notice when they are coming because they release bubbles as they swim. It's beautiful. They make a beautiful noise, the air bubbles. And the dolphins can be just beside your boat and look at you. It's very amazing. You will see."

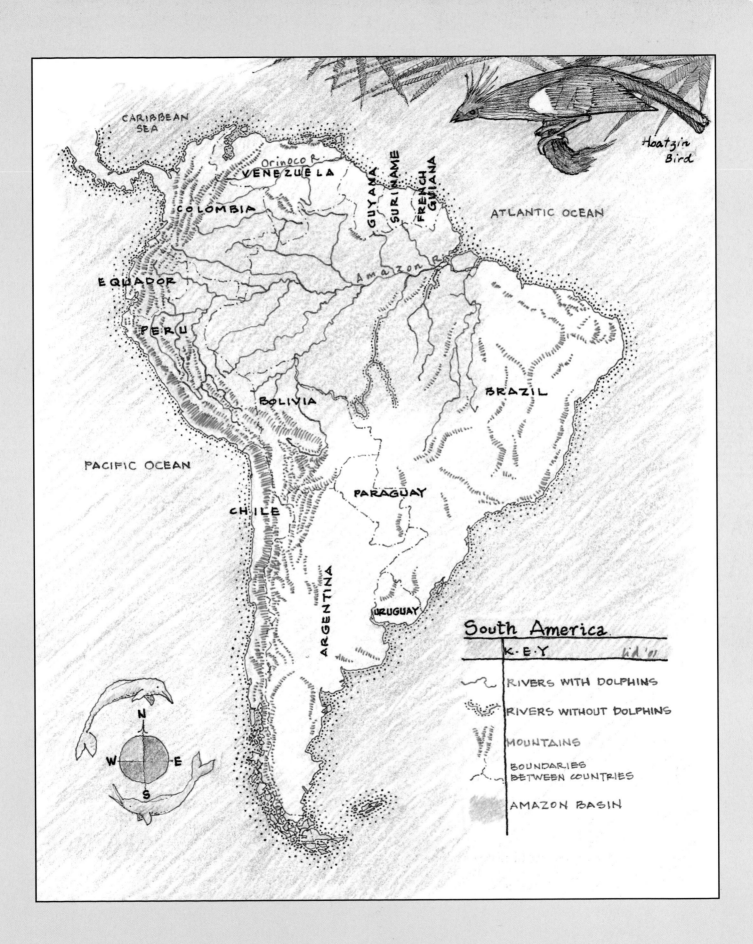

CARIBBEAN SEA

Orinoco R

VENEZUELA

COLOMBIA

GUYANA

SURINAME

FRENCH GUIANA

ATLANTIC OCEAN

Amazon R

EQUADOR

PERU

PACIFIC OCEAN

BOLIVIA

BRAZIL

PARAGUAY

CHILE

ARGENTINA

URUGUAY

N
W E
S

Hoatzin Bird

South America

K·E·Y   lid '01

~~~ RIVERS WITH DOLPHINS

~~~ RIVERS WITHOUT DOLPHINS

~~~ MOUNTAINS

~~~ BOUNDARIES BETWEEN COUNTRIES

AMAZON BASIN

But no one knows how many pink dolphins exist in the Amazon or how their travels change from the wet season to the dry season. No one knows when their mating season is. No one knows if they live in big groups or in small families of just mothers and babies or if this varies from place to place.

There are many mysteries to solve.

You'd better get to it!

BACK TO THE DRAWING BOARD—OR, IN YOUR CASE, BACK TO THE CANOE.

Maybe you will still get only little glimpses of dolphins. Maybe you will see only the flash of a tail, the top of a head.

But there's still a way to make sense out of what you see.

Scientists like Vera are always counting, measuring, and sorting things into categories. A single record may not tell you much. It might not seem to matter that a dolphin surfaced at 10:41 A.M. But if you keep measuring, recording, and sorting, all your measurements, like the tiny dots that make up a newspaper photograph, eventually may form a picture—or, like the individual letters in these words, may tell a story.

Time to pack a notebook, a pencil, and a stopwatch in your backpack, along with your

sun hat, poncho, insect repellent, and drinking water.

You'll watch for pink flashes on the water. You'll look for bubbles near your canoe. You'll listen for splashes and gasps of breath. You'll write down the time and the weather. You'll record any dolphins seen close together and those seen far apart. And anytime you see something special happening, you'll record it in detail, just as if you were writing a story.

Because you *are* writing a story—one measurement at a time.

The Scientist and the Shaman

ONE WEEK LATER, YOU'VE COLLECTED DOZENS AND DOZENS OF OBSERVATIONS. Your data sheets carefully record each pink dolphin sighting with time, date, weather, and other observations. And a picture is starting to emerge.

Some days you record 160 surfacings in a single hour. There is definitely more than one dolphin out there—some days you are certain there are at least five.

And at least four times, you have seen a mother and a baby. They surfaced at the same moment within fifty yards of the canoe, a big pink mother and a little gray young one. They were so close to each other they could have touched, flipper to flipper, like a human parent

holding a child's hand. Once the baby surfaced and slowly rolled over. You could see a chubby pink belly and paddle-shaped flippers spread wide apart—like a person floating on his back with arms outstretched.

You've also been able to see from your data that there are certain times when the dolphins are more active. They tend to splash and blow louder and more frequently for a half-hour or so, then rest for about the same amount of time.

At noon the dolphins often seem to be taking a siesta. In fact, you may have seen one sleeping. At the shallow end of the lake, you recorded a dolphin slowly rising to take a breath, then sinking back down gently—and then, a few minutes later, rising in exactly the same spot. You timed it: the dolphin stayed in the same spot for eight minutes. Actually, dolphins don't sleep the way we do; they simply rest one side of the brain at a time. They even sleep with one eye open. They don't really catnap—they whale-nap.

Studying the dolphins has given you a chance to look in on lots of other lives, too.

One morning, on your way out to the dolphin lake, you were amazed to see that someone had strung a badminton net between two treetops poking up through the water. The net glistened in the morning dew. Who would put up a badminton net in the middle of the water?

Moises knew. It wasn't a badminton net after all—it was a giant spider web! It was made, he told you, by perhaps as many as ten fishing spiders. They probably worked on it all night. And the giant net is strong enough to catch fish—which was exactly the idea.

The Amazon has its share of giants, but it has miniature creatures, too. Good thing you

brought your binoculars. Without them, you could never have seen what Moises spotted with his sharp Amazon eyes. It took you a while, but finally you focused on the face of a little, wide-eyed sprite clinging to a branch with orange hands. No wonder you had trouble seeing this tiny monkey, called a pygmy marmoset. It is less than four inches long, including the ringed black and beige tail.

You've found you're not the only one watching. You are being watched, too. One day, on the way out to the lake, Moises pointed to something high in a tree. Looking down at you with a brown-eyed stare was a red uakari monkey, clearly observing your progress. (Wonder if he was taking notes, too?)

It's called a red uakari because of its bright red face. Because of its auburn coat, it looks sort of like a miniature orangutan. But Moises says the local people say it looks like a sunburned tourist!

Monkeys aren't the only ones watching you. One day you passed a school on stilts. During recess, some little girls were playing in a canoe. But when they saw you, they abandoned their game for something more interesting:

ABOVE: *Ten or so fishing spiders worked together all night to weave this web, which is as big as a badminton net.*
BELOW: *A red uakari monkey.*

47

A tamarin monkey.

"Vamamos a ver el gringo!" said one. That means "Let's go watch the foreigner, the gringo!" They canoed over and stared at you carefully for several minutes, smiling shyly.

Every day when you leave the lodge, and in the evening when you go back, you pass the houses where the schoolchildren and their parents live at the edge of the river. This gives you an idea. These people live with dolphins right at their doorsteps. What have they observed about your study subjects? Surely their observations would shed light on your own.

Could you arrange to talk with some of the people about the dolphins? "Sure," says Moises. The local people, he says, are eager to invite you into their homes. They're happy to share with you what they know.

"BUENOS DÍAS!" SAYS JUAN HUANAKIRI, AS YOU CLIMB THE LADDER up to the stilt house he built at the edge of the river. He and his wife, Ilda, motion for you to sit on the springy floor with them. They offer you a handsome mat to sit on, woven by Ilda from palm fronds.

Almost everything in the house the family has made by hand from the riches of the forest around them. To you, at first, the jungle seemed scary—full of unseen snakes who might bite you, thorns that might prick you, mosquitoes who suck your blood, and piranhas who might try to eat you. But to the local people here, the rain forest is like a generous mother who gives them everything they need.

Juan cut the beams for his family's house from the red wood of the capirona tree. The roof is thatched with the leaves of the yarina palm. The house is clean and spacious. In the rafters of the ceiling, you can see items tucked neatly out of the way: Juan's blowguns and hunting spears; jars of medicines made from plants; some wooden bowls; a big drum made from the hide of a peccary, or wild pig.

"Please, I want to learn more about the *bufeo colorado*," you say in English. Juan speaks Spanish and Quechua, an Indian language, so Moises translates. Here is Juan's reply:

"The people here have a belief about the *bufeo colorado*. They live in our world, but they also live beneath the water in a more beautiful world. We call it the Encante. The *bufeo* is boss of this magical world. And the bufeo has many magical powers."

And then he begins to tell a story:

Once, in a village like this one, there lived a very beautiful girl named Cecelia. One day when she was washing clothes in the river, a bufeo swam by. He saw how pretty Cecelia was. He appreciated how hard she worked washing the clothes. He heard her humming a pretty song as she worked.

The bufeo fell in love.

The girl didn't notice the dolphin. Day after day he swam by, hoping to see her and hoping she would notice how much he liked her. But she didn't. She was thinking of other things: weeding the garden, making a stew for dinner. And she thought about her husband, a young man who worked in the forest.

One day her husband went into the forest to work. Sometimes when he went away he had to stay for months, even years. But this time he came back that very night, and she was glad. He brought her many kinds of beautiful fish—some she had never seen before. She made a tasty stew, and the couple had a feast.

Juan and Ilda Huanakiri.

In the morning, though, Cecelia's husband left again. He came back that night and again brought more delicious fish.

Things went on like this month after happy month. Then one day, when her husband

Almost all of the furnishings in Juan and Ilda's house came from the forest, including this ocelot skin.

came home, he didn't bring any fish. "Why don't you have any fish tonight, my husband?" asked the beautiful Cecelia. Her husband was surprised. "I never brought you any fish," he answered. "Why, I've been away in the forest for a year."

What had happened?

Juan says that was just what the husband wanted to know!

To find out, the husband went to the wisest man he knew: the village shaman. A shaman is like a combination of a doctor and a priest. He knows how to make medicines from jungle plants to cure sick people. And he also knows the spirit world of the jungle. He can hear the voices of the plants and animals, the fishes and the dolphins. Sometimes the plant spirits tell the shaman how to cure sick people and how to make special medicines. Sometimes the animal spirits tell him where to hunt to find food. And sometimes the dolphin spirits reveal secrets about the beautiful underwater world of the Encante—a world only the shaman can visit.

In a trance, the shaman visited the enchanted underwater kingdom, where there was music, dancing, feasts, and festivals. Caimans and catfish, otters and arauanas, piranhas and pirarucus, all danced and sang together in a peaceful world of plenty—a world ruled by magical pink dolphins.

A shaman.

There the shaman met the dolphin who had fallen in love with Cecelia. And he found out what had happened.

"The *bufeo colorado* has powerful magic," Juan says again. Lonely for Cecelia's love, each night the pink dolphin left his watery world behind. Each night when her husband was away, the dolphin had come up on the land and magically changed his shape. His flippers turned into hands, his tail into feet. The dolphin transformed himself into the very image of Cecelia's husband.

Dolphins and humans, you see, are not that different after all.

Now that was some story!

You leave the Huanakiris' house wondering: Do Juan and Ilda really believe that story? Can pink dolphins change into something else? Are they really magic?

But you're about to hear an even stranger tale—this one from a scientist.

Time Travel

ONE DAY WHEN YOU RETURN FROM A MORNING OF DATA-COLLECTING, THERE'S a new visitor to the lodge.

Meet Gary Galbreath. He's a professor of biology at Northwestern University, near Chicago, Illinois. His special interest is paleontology, the study of life in the prehistoric past. That's one reason he has made the trip to the rain forest here.

You look around at his luggage. Has he brought a time machine to Peru?

No, he explains—he doesn't need one. "You could say this place takes you back in time," he says.

Paleontologist and time-traveler Gary Galbreath.

There are creatures living here in the Amazon who look like prehistoric animals of many millions of years ago. These creatures, Gary says, "are like windows through which you can glimpse lost worlds."

They can take you back to a time when the Amazon's caimans grew as big as *Tyrannosaurus rex*. They can remind you of long-lost creatures like the *borhyaenids* (BORE-hi-EEN-ids) of 15 million years ago. These mammals, the most numerous meat-eaters of that time, had sharp teeth like wolves. The mothers carried their babies in a pouch, the way possums and kangaroos do. The Amazon's forests were full of six-foot-tall "terror birds." These creatures had feathers and beaks, Gary explains, but paleontologists never found any wings. What they found instead astonished everyone: these giant birds used their arms not to fly but to grab their prey—they had hands tipped with daggerlike claws.

Many creatures here preserve a sort of memory of when the world was much younger— a time when the ancient Amazon itself was new.

And one of those creatures is the pink dolphin.

Ready for time travel? All you have to do is join Gary in the canoe.

GARY HAS DREAMED ABOUT THE LIVES OF PREHISTORIC ANIMALS EVER SINCE HE played with plastic dinosaurs as a kid. (He still has some of those dinos on his dresser at home today.) "But dinosaurs weren't the only strange and wonderful creatures in the prehistoric past," Gary tells you.

Want to meet some of the others?

Your first stop is the Devonian era, 400 million years back in time. To get there, all you have to do is visit the floating house next door.

Juan Salas, who works at the lodge, lives in the floating house. He has just returned from a morning of fishing—and he's brought a special present for you and Gary: a fish covered in bony plates like black armor. In fact, it's called an armored catfish. "It looks like a fossil we have at the Field Museum in Chicago!" Gary says. "Only smaller."

The fossil fish, which Gary knows well, is called *Dunkleosteus* (dunkle-OS-tee-us). Its skull is several feet long. *Dunkleosteus* belonged to a group of fishes called the placoderms (PLAH-koe-derms). *Placo* means plate; *derm* means skin. "They were covered with plate armor, espe-

The armored catfish recalls the monster fish of Devonian seas.

cially on the front. Several kinds of placoderms even had little plates covering part of the eye sockets." Gary says.

Why did they need all that armor?

"Back in the Devonian," explains Gary, "the sea was full of hungry monsters. Among them were huge, eel-like sharks with weird jaws. The upper jaw was like a Frisbee covered with teeth. They rammed their prey and cut the body in half!"

Those monsters are gone now—fortunately for us—and so are the placoderms.

They went extinct, just as the dinosaurs did. But there are still fish in the waters here that remind you of them—like this armored catfish.

These ancient forms can persist here because rain forests are almost like living museums. "The rain forest is one of the most ancient natural habitats on earth," Gary tells you. Wood-

ABOVE: *A fungus that glows.*
BELOW: *A rain-forest flower.*

lands like most of North America's forests appeared on earth 33 million years ago. Grasslands evolved 23 million years ago. Pine forests didn't exist until about 5 million years ago. "But rain forests much like this one go back 100 million years. And tropical forests, even though the trees were very different then, go back even further—several hundred million years."

As you canoe through the flooded forest, Gary can help you see the world as it once was.

"Three hundred million years ago, a good part of the world was like this," he says. "Much of the world was flooded like this forest, covered with huge swamps." This era, the Carboniferous, is also known as the Coal Age. The flooding knocked over trees, and after millions of years the trees turned into the coal that supplies energy to many power plants today.

There were differences, of course, between the first rain forests of the Carboniferous and this one.

"There were no flowering plants then. Many of the trees had scaly bark and little scaly leaves. There were no beetles or butterflies but plenty of dragonflies and cockroaches," Gary says.

You can still see lots of roaches and dragonflies in the Amazon today. In fact, dragonflies are all around you now, glimmering in the hot, still air.

"Now imagine that their wings are as big as a sea gull's," Gary says. "That's what they looked like back then." In your imagination, you can begin to see the world as it was in the Carboniferous. Ferns curled skyward, growing into fifty-foot trees. Giant amphibians lurked in the shallows. Imagine if the little salamander under that leaf were as big as a man! Millipedes—like the one coiled in the tree over there—grew six feet long.

There were no dinosaurs yet in the Carboniferous. But soon you will see one. For now, you're bound for the Jurassic. This is Gary's favorite era, the time when the dinosaurs reigned supreme.

With Moises at the helm, you are headed to Caiman Lake. Moises has a surprise for you. And to find it, you have to look up in the trees.

There! Gary focuses his binoculars on the top of a spindly tree poking up out of the water. And now you see it, too: a strange, chicken-sized bird with an orange crest and red eyes. It hisses at you just like a reptile. And it is a sort of reptile, as the dinosaurs were. "In fact, most scientists agree that birds are what became of the dinosaurs," Gary explains. "Birds are the dinosaurs who evolved to fly. When the other dinosaurs went extinct at the end of the Cretaceous, 65 million years ago, the birds sailed on.

"Just think," he says, "at your window at home you might have a dinosaur feeder. And for Thanksgiving dinner, you're really eating a dinosaur."

The bird above you now, called a hoatzin, is particularly dinolike. It sits next to its mate on a nest of sticks. Inside are their babies, who have reptilelike claws on their wings.

There once were dinosaurs with wings. The first one was called *Archaeopteryx* (ar-key-OP-ter-icks). Its Latin name means ancient wing. It is the earliest bird we know—a dinosaur who was part bird, part reptile. It, too, had claws on the wings, even as an adult. Its long jaws had tiny teeth. The tail, long and bony, trailed behind the dino-bird when it flew—like a lizard in flight.

"The hoatzin is not a 'missing link' between *Archaeopteryx* and modern birds," says Gary, "but all modern birds may be descendants of *Archaeopteryx*."

You can't help but be reminded of *Archaeopteryx* as you look at the strange creature staring down at you now. The hoatzin is about the same size as its "ancient-wing" ancestor: about two feet long and weighing two pounds. The bird above you also has a long tail, the feathers streaked brown and yellowish. It stares down at you with red eyes set in a blue face.

"Wow," says Gary softly. "This is really primeval!"

And so is the creature who greets you with a gasp on your way back to the lodge: the pink dolphin. The spray in the air from its breath is all you see of it today—that and a short glimpse of pink.

It's so frustrating trying to study an animal you spot for only a few moments. But Gary understands that. "It's like working with fossils," says the paleontologist. When digging up fossils, it's very unusual to find a whole skeleton. Usually you get just little pieces. "There are entire creatures from the past we know from only a single tooth," he explains.

That was the case with the first prehistoric whales—the ancestors of the pink dolphins and all the other whales. Gary explains that the first fossils were unearthed in places that once were shallow seas but are now dry land, in Pakistan, Egypt, and Texas. No one was sure what they looked like, because scientists had only pieces of the skeletons. Each bone was a precious glimpse at an otherwise vanished life.

The ancestors of the whales were land mammals, Gary explains. But how did a mammal whose ancestors had lived for millions of years on land slowly change into one who lived in the water like a fish? For many years, the evolution of whales and dolphins was one of the deepest mysteries of paleontology.

Only recently did scientists find the answer. It's a story so fantastic that if there were no fossils to prove it, no one would believe it.

Gary's story could begin the way fairy tales do: "Once upon a time."

The time was 50 million years ago. The epoch was the Eocene—the Dawn Age, for it was the beginning of the Age of Mammals. And at that time, explains Gary, there were whales who walked.

Whales who walk! It sounds as impossible as dolphins who dance. But it's true, and the truth is literally cast in stone in the fossilized remains of whales with legs. In 1993 a paleontologist named Hans Thewissen of Northeastern Ohio University was digging for fossils in an area of Pakistan that was full of fossil clams. It was once a shallow sea—a good

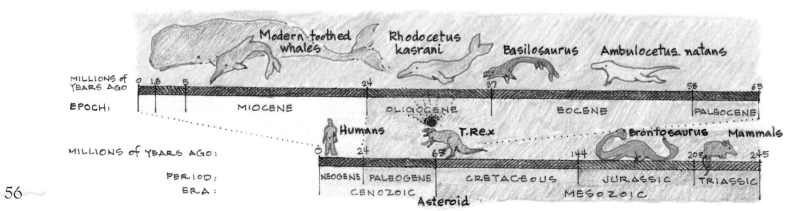

56

place to look for fossil whales. And there the paleontologist found the bones of a creature that was definitely an early whale, one who had lived 50 million years ago. Piece by piece, a picture of the ancient whale came together, as Hans Thewissen dug up each bone. The whale had no front legs; in their place were front flippers. The backbone and ribs showed that the whale was probably about as big as a male sea lion. It may have weighed 660 pounds. But instead of back flippers like a sea lion or a fluked tail like a whale, this early

Dino-bird: the young of the hoatzin have claws on their wings.

whale still had legs. And at the end of its legs it had feet—tipped with hooves like a pig!

Hans named the new fossil *Ambulocetus natans*—*ambulo* comes from the Latin word for walking; *cetus,* for cetacean; and *natans,* from the word for swimming. He had found the Walking Whale Who Swims.

Here was the "missing link" between the land-dwelling mammal from which whales descended and the oceangoing creatures that whales would become.

But then there was a gap in the fossil record, explains Gary—one that lasted 10 million years, until the end of the next epoch, the Oligocene. The next whale fossils we have are skeletons of a creature who looked much like our pink dolphins today. They have no back legs; they have broad, flippered hands; and they are perfectly adapted to life in the water.

"The group of toothed whales that gave rise to pink dolphins is an ancient one," Gary says. "Indeed, the pink dolphins and the Amazon evolved together." Many scientists think that the ancestors of the pink dolphins swam into the Amazon from the Pacific Ocean perhaps 15 million years ago.

Today, as you can see from a map, the Amazon flows into the Atlantic, on the east side of the continent. But 15 million years ago, before the slow but violent rise of the Andes

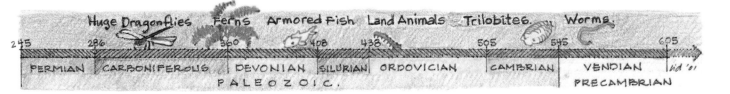

Huge Dragonflies   Ferns   Armored Fish   Land Animals   Trilobites   Worms

245   286   360   408   438   505   545   605

PERMIAN | CARBONIFEROUS | DEVONIAN | SILURIAN | ORDOVICIAN | CAMBRIAN | VENDIAN | hid 'oi

PALEOZOIC   PRECAMBRIAN

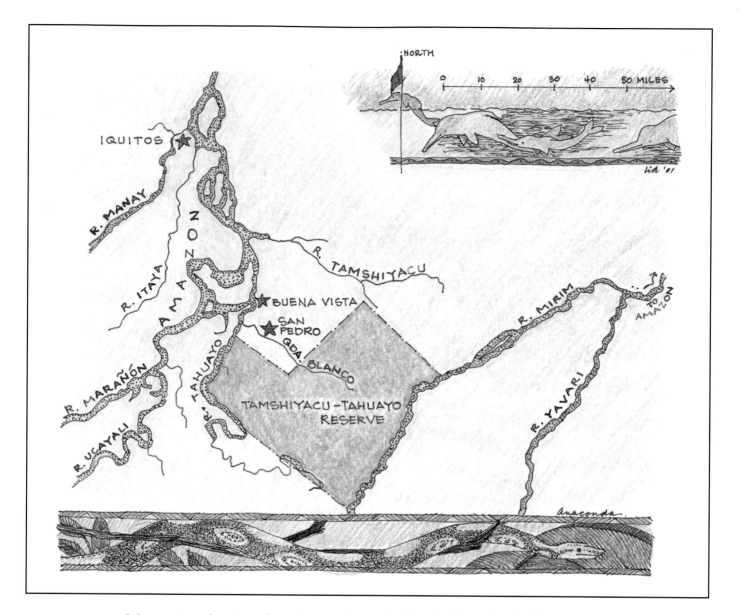

Mountains, the river flowed west, into the Pacific. Just think: the pink dolphins may have been here longer than the Andes mountains.

"You know," says Gary, "piecing together the prehistoric past is like piecing together the lives of the dolphins you are watching. There are always gaps to fill in. But the next big chapter in the story of the pink dolphins is what lies ahead." Today the Amazon is changing faster than it has ever changed before. Maybe, Gary suggests, the pink dolphins can help you see the future as well as the past.

Into the Future

CAN THE TIMELESS AMAZON REALLY BE CHANGING?

One day at the lodge, you get a glimpse of the future firsthand. Your lunch is interrupted by the loud noise of a big boat motor. You leave the long wooden dining table and go out on the porch to see.

It's an enormous boat from Iquitos, longer than fifteen canoes. It's towing a raft of more than fifty giant logs—more than fifty trees.

Throughout the Amazon, trees are being felled at an appalling rate. Every hour of every

day, according to some scientists' calculations, an area of Amazon rain forest as large as 630 football fields is cut down!

Gary explains that the trees are cut down for many reasons. Sometimes the forest is cleared to make pastures for cattle ranches. The clearings are so huge that the forest can't grow back. To raise cattle and make enough meat for just one hamburger, an area of rain forest about the size of your kitchen is permanently destroyed.

Sometimes trees are cut to sell as logs for making fancy, expensive furniture. Mahogany is one of the fine woods cut from the rain forest.

But most of the trees cut in the Amazon, Gary says, go to make paper, packaging material, and particleboard—the stuff used to block up the broken windows of abandoned buildings.

"What a waste of beautiful forest!" says Gary. Just think of the uses the forest animals had for those trees. Hoatzins and oropendulas and antbirds built their nests there. Parrots and bamboo rats and big spiders lived in the hollows. Bats slept hanging upside down from the branches. Deer, wild pigs, and other animals ate the trees' fruits. And fish, too, eat the fruits when they drop into the water—fish that the pink dolphins depend on for their dinners. Vines, ferns, cactuses, orchids, and bromeliads teeming with hundreds of creatures coiled around and perched on the branches of the trees. The local people need the trees, too, Moises adds. Remember your first canoe trip to the dolphin lake? Moises had begun to explain how local people make medicines from the leaves, bark, and sap of the trees. Then, at Juan and Ilda's house, you saw that local people need the trees to build their homes, make their blowguns and drums, weave their sitting mats. And they eat the fruits of the trees, too—like that pineapple you ate for dessert, as well as other rain-forest fruits you don't get to see in supermarkets at home, with names like aguaje (uh-GWAH-hay), which looks sort of like a pinecone and tastes like Gouda cheese.

But to the people who live there, the rain forest is more than just a free store full of things they need. Remember Juan's story about Cecelia, the shaman, and the dolphin? The shamans of the Amazon believe that the spirits of the forests and the rivers have knowledge and power that people need to survive. The people respect and honor both the land and the water. The rain forest, to them, is a magical place, alive with souls and spirits not unlike our own.

And that's exactly why the people who live near the lodge don't let big timber companies or rich cattle ranchers ruin these forests. "That boat, that's not from around here," Moises says. The rain forest near the villages you pass every day on your way to watch dolphins is protected—and in a very unusual way.

In 1991, 800,000 acres of rain forest outside these villages became the Tamshiyacu-Tahuayo Community Reserve, Gary explains. It was the first of its kind in Peru: a reserve that is run by and for the local people, who use the rain forest's resources to protect the forest and its wildlife.

"People want to protect the reserve because an important part of their livelihood comes from it," Gary explains. "They want to sustain it so it can sustain them."

The villagers saw rich outsiders raiding their forest—cutting down trees, hunting the animals to sell at the market in Iquitos. They saw big ships coming to their lakes and taking away all the fish. They saw the future: if things continued like that, there wouldn't be any fish, any trees, or any dolphins. But they saw another future, too, one in which the rain forest was safe. And they decided to try to make that future a reality.

But they needed help. And that's where the Rainforest Conservation Fund came in.

The Rainforest Conservation Fund, based in Chicago, helped the people in the Amazon persuade their lawmakers to create the reserve in the first place. The fund pays the expenses of scientists who investigate the lives of the animals who live there to find out what they animals need to survive. It supports the people in their efforts to keep outsiders from fishing, hunting, and cutting trees in the reserve. And its scientists and foresters help the people police themselves, too.

The local people know that even in their own community, people might take more than they need, cut too many trees, kill too many animals. So, on advice from the scientists, they have agreed among themselves to limit their hunting. Instead of cutting down trees from the forest, they plant special gardens at the edge of the forest called *chacras* (CHA-kras). The gardens grow native Amazon trees. Some are grown for their fruits, others provide leaves for medicines, and a few are grown for timber. When the people cut a tree down, they plant a new one. And if they move away from that place, they leave behind a young forest instead of an abandoned cornfield.

The Rainforest Conservation Fund helps the people find the best ways to plant and grow the trees. It also provides legal advice so the villagers can persuade lawmakers in Iquitos to enforce the laws protecting the animals and plants in the reserve from outsiders.

How does Gary know so much about the reserve? Because he was president of the Rainforest Conservation Fund when it took on the Tamshiyacu-Tahuayo Community Reserve as a project. And he is still a volunteer officer of the fund today.

"I am very sad there are not tyrannosaurs, stegosaurs, glyptodonts today," Gary says. "All of them I wish I could resurrect." Of course, he can't do that—any more than he could have stopped their extinction, millions of years before he was born. But, by volunteering to work with a conservation organization, today he can help protect this ancient, primordial Amazon rain-forest world and its creatures.

"We don't have to lose the rain-forest battle," he says, as the logging boat disappears into the distance.

His words make you remember something Vera said to you on the shortwave: "We have the choice," she said, "to protect it or not."

Aguaje fruit is sold at the market in Iquitos.

AFTER TWO WEEKS, IT'S TIME TO LEAVE THE RAINFOREST LODGE. YOU PACK UP your notebooks, now full of observations. You pack up your binoculars. You pack up your clothes and your water bottles. You pack your camera and the rolls and rolls of film you have taken of the people and plants and animals you met here.

It's a long ride back to Iquitos in the motorboat. On the trip, you watch the river grow wider. The tributaries braid into the Amazon, until it looks as wide as a sea. The farther you travel, the more changes you notice: the small canoes, like those you saw near the lodge, aren't the only boat traffic. Look: on a wide expanse of river, a tugboat is pushing two giant barges loaded with a herd of yellow bulldozers. They look like angry dragons.

Moises tells you the bulldozers are headed for the Pastaza River, where American companies are drilling for oil. Sometimes there are terrible accidents at these projects. Moises

remembers that in 1992 a major oil spill in the neighboring country of Ecuador released 27,000 gallons of oil into the Napo River—the river along which Moises grew up. "Many, many animals died," Moises says. "Fish, turtles—dolphins, too."

A sad picture forms in your mind as you think about those dead creatures. Is this their future? Or is another future possible? Which do you choose?

Just then, a pink dolphin surfaces right in front of your boat. As if by magic, it seems, the dolphin showed up to help you answer that question.

Perhaps these encantados really are magic, just as Juan and Ilda said.

After all, look at where the dolphins have led you. They led you to swim in an underwater jungle. They led you up into the treetops, where you discovered a whole leafy world you never could have imagined. They led you to experiment with the world of science. They led you into the local people's stories and myths. And by following them you have had a chance to travel back into the past—and to consider the future.

The dolphin's low pink fin seems to linger for a minute on the water's surface, like a kite floating on the wind. And then it's gone.

How This Book Was Researched

EVERYTHING IN THIS BOOK IS TRUE.

Every scene really happened. All the people, places, and animals in it are real. And every word quoted in this book was really spoken.

I made four expeditions to the Amazon in 1998 while researching a book for adult readers called *Journey of the Pink Dolphins: An Amazon Quest*. I visited four different research sites in Brazil and Peru. The longest trip lasted two months; the shortest was two weeks.

In Manaus, Brazil, I met and interviewed Dr. Vera da Silva, the pink dolphin researcher. Vera was extremely generous with her time and knowledge. During my two trips to Peru, I stayed at the Rainforest Lodge, operated by Amazonia Expeditions at the edge of the Tamshiyacu-Tahuayo Community Reserve in Loreto Province. Here I met Moises Chavez, my wonderful guide, and Juan and Ilda Huanakiri, who told me stories about the pink dolphins. On my second trip to the lodge, it was my great fortune to meet Dr. Gary Galbreath, who took me time-traveling millions of years in the past.

Many other people helped me, too. Even though you did not meet them in these pages, their knowledge and kindness enrich this book.

They include Nildon Athaide; Dr. Paul Beaver; Selinda Chiquoine; Lilla, Jane, and Kate Cabot; Heather Cummings; Isabelle Druant; Amy Flynn; Sarah Jane Freymann; Lucineldo Marino Goncalvez; Dr. Jon Green; Dr. Peter Henderson; Maria do Soccoro D'antona Machado; Howard Mansfield; Keila Marinho; Miriam Marmontel; Dave Meyer; Greg Neise; Steve Nordlinger; Bob and Judith Oksner; Jim Penn; Ricardo Pipa; Andrea Piris; Dr. Mark Plotkin; Denise Roy; Juan Salas; Dr. Joy Schochet; Ronis da Silviera; Jorge Soplin; Agusuto Teran; and Elizabeth Marshall Thomas.

Everywhere I traveled in the Amazon, I met kind and knowledgeable souls. They answered my questions. They offered advice. They told me their stories. They welcomed me into their homes. Some translated for me. Some piloted speedboats and canoes.

Some were fishermen, some were scientists, some were shamans, some were dancers.

And many of them were dolphins.

I thank them all.

A Note on the Photographs

DIANNE TAYLOR-SNOW IS A CALIFORNIA-BASED PHOTOGRAPHER WHO travels the world taking pictures of animals and jungles. She accompanied me on all but one of the four expeditions to the Amazon.

Besides the photos of pink dolphins in the wild, she has also taken some close-ups to give you an idea of what the dolphins look like face to face. These photos are of Chuckles, North America's only captive pink river dolphin, whom we met at the Pittsburgh Zoo in Pennsylvania.

Dianne Taylor-Snow

To Visit the Amazon

YOU AND YOUR FAMILY OR SCHOOL GROUP ARE WELCOME AT THE RAIN-forest Lodge right outside the Tamshiyacu-Tahuayo Community Reserve, where the events described in this book take place. The company that runs it has special programs for kids. They also generously support the Rainforest Conservation Fund, helping local people protect the beautiful land around the lodge. To find out about trips, you may contact:

Amazonia Expeditions

18500 Gulf Boulevard, No. 201

Indian Shores, FL 33785

Telephone: 1 800 262 9669

Or visit the Web site: www.perujungle.com.

To Help Save the Amazon

YOU CAN BECOME A MEMBER OF THE RAINFOREST CONSERVATION FUND, WHICH SUP-ports the Tamshiyacu-Tahuayo Community Reserve. Learn more about the fund and its work by writing to:

Rainforest Conservation Fund

2038 North Clark Street

Chicago, IL 60614

Or visit its Web site at: www.rainforestconservation.org.

THE AMAZON CONSERVATION TEAM, FOUNDED BY DR. MARK Plotkin, works to conserve local knowledge of plants and plant medicines and traditional knowledge all over the Amazon. You can become a member and learn more by writing to:

Amazon Conservation Team

2330 Wilson Boulevard

Arlington, VA 22201

Visit its Web site at: www.ethnobotany.org.

Amazon Index: Some Startling Statistics

Length of the Amazon River: 4,000 miles

Size of the Amazon jungle: 2.5 million square miles

Kinds of vanilla orchids in the Amazon: 250

Percentage of plants, by weight, growing on trees as epiphytes in the Amazon: 40 percent

Species of fish in the Mississippi River: 250

Species of fish in the Congo River: 1,000

Species of fish in the Amazon: more than 2,500

Number of teeth in a dolphin's mouth: 130

Weight of a large, adult male pink dolphin: 400 pounds

Number of fingers inside a dolphin's front flipper: 5

Years a pink dolphin can live in captivity: more than 30

Percentage of the Amazon rain forest that has already been destroyed: 15 percent

Brazil's rank among all the world's countries that are losing rain forest each year: first

Number of Indian tribes that have gone extinct in Brazil since 1900: more than 90

Amount of Brazilian rain forest destroyed each year: 5,800 square miles

Additional rain forest "thinned" through logging each year: 4,200 square miles

Protected land in Peru's Tamshiyacu-Tahuayo Community Reserve: 800,000 acres

Strange Lives: A Cast of Amazon Characters

Arauana: a long, silvery fish who can leap six feet out of the water and grab prey out of the trees.

Armored catfish: a heavy, black fish covered with armorlike scales. Local people say that when the pink dolphin turns into a person and shows up at dances, he wears armored catfish on his feet to cover up his tail flukes.

Bushmaster: the world's largest pit viper and the most fearsome snake in the Amazon. It grows to fifteen feet and stabs its victims repeatedly with massive fangs.

Boto, a.k.a. bufeo colorado or encantado or *Inia geoffrensis:* the pink dolphin.

Bromeliad: a plant related to pineapples, with spiky, overlapping leaves that can form a bowl, catching rainwater. More than 500 species of creatures can live in the rainwater captured in a bromeliad's bowl.

Caimans: crocodiles of the Amazon, unchanged for millions of years.

Hairy megalomorphs: several species of big, hairy spiders like tarantulas, whose belly can grow as large as a tangerine. Their main defense is the hair on their legs. If the hairs touch you, you will itch like crazy. The spiders sometimes pull out their hair with their legs and throw it.

Hoatzin: orange-crested, chicken-sized bird with a blue face and red eyes. The young have claws on their wings.

Mata-mata: a large turtle who lures prey into its open mouth with a piece of flesh on its tongue that looks just like a worm.

Pirarucu: a big Amazon fish who grows teeth on its tongue. Local river people dry pirarucu tongues and use them like cheese graters.

Poison dart frogs: several species of frogs who have poisons in their skin so toxic that local people use the chemicals to tip their arrows and kill prey faster.

Sack-winged bat: handsome little bats who have a strange courtship ritual. The males attract females by spitting into their armpits. The spit ferments and produces an odor that drives the females wild.

Weird Whale Facts

World's Largest Animal Ever: The 90-foot, 100-ton blue whale is bigger than the biggest dinosaur who ever lived. An adult blue whale grows as long as three school buses and weighs more than a thousand people. Its tongue alone weighs as much as an elephant, and some of its blood vessels are so big you could stand up inside them.

Whales Who Sing: Humpback whales compose a long, complex series of underwater chirps, clicks, *whoos*, trills, *yups*, and cries that scientists have only recently recognized as songs. Like our songs and those of birds, whale songs have a beginning, a middle, and an end, and they can last half an hour. Importantly all the whales in a given area sing the same song—but it changes from year to year.

Toothless Wonder: The biggest creature who ever lived has no teeth. Instead of munching its food, the blue whale strains it like a sieve. This kind of whale has, instead of teeth, hanging plates of baleen, made of the same stuff as your fingernails, which hangs down from the upper jaw like fringe on a lampshade. The whale filters water through the baleen to strain out the tiny shrimplike krill and other tiny animals that are its only food. Other baleen whales include the humpback whale, the gray whale, and the bowhead whale.

Unicorn Whale: One kind of whale, the narwhal, has only one tooth, which grows from the upper jaw. It sticks way out on the front of its face like a unicorn's horn. Only the males have this special tusk, and no one knows what it's for.

Hold Your Nose: Instead of holding their nose when they dive underwater, whales shut their

blowholes with special muscles. A dolphin can shut its blowhole faster than a camera shutter snaps shut.

World's Rarest Whale: The baiji is a Chinese river whale who looks much like the pink Amazon dolphin (except that it's light blue). Living only in the polluted Yangtze River, this dolphin now has new woes to contend with: huge hydroelectric dams that disrupt the flow of its river. There may be less than thirty of these animals left in the world, and scientists fear they are doomed to extinction.

Unsolved Mysteries

Many questions remain unanswered about the pink dolphins of the Amazon. Here are just a few. Perhaps you will be the one to solve them!

Do pink dolphins live in different areas in the wet season and the dry season? If so, why?

When do pink dolphins mate?

How long do pink dolphins in the wild live?

How many pink dolphins are there in the Amazon?

What sorts of groups do pink dolphins form? How long do these associations last? What forms the basis for their bonds?

What are the main threats to the pink dolphins' survival in today's changing Amazon? How would you protect them against those threats?

Pink dolphins have excellent hearing and fine eyesight, but how important are their senses of taste and smell? Other than echolocation, do they have senses we don't have?

People tell many stories about dolphins in the Amazon. Do they have a common theme? Is there a factual scientific basis for these beliefs?

Do pink dolphins have territories, as tigers and wolves do? If so, how do they decide upon and defend territorial boundaries?

Many of the threats to the pink dolphins' rain forests and rivers today bring us products we use in North America. Oil drilling brings heat for our homes and gas for our cars. Woodcutting brings packaging for our goods. Gold mining gives us fine jewelry. What can we do in our everyday lives to ease our demands on the rain forests?

Some Further Reading

ABOUT THE AMAZON

The Amazon, by Julia Waterlow (Austin, Tex.: Raintree Steck-Vaughn, 1993).

In stories and pictures, this book provides an overview of the Amazon River, its jungles, towns, people, and animals, as well as threats to its environment.

The Great Kapok Tree, by Lynne Cherry (Orlando, Fla.: Harcourt, 1990).

In this story set in the Amazon rain forest, a man is chopping down a great kapok tree. When he puts down his ax and rests, he dreams that the animals who live in the tree plead with him not to destroy their world. The illustrations are as lush as the rain forest and contain just as much information as the words.

The Shaman's Apprentice: A Tale of the Amazon Rain Forest, by Lynne Cherry and Mark Plotkin (New York: Gulliver Green/Harcourt Brace, 1998).

A Tirio Indian shaman passes his vast knowledge of the forest's healing secrets to a young initiate—and just in time. This is a fictionalized account of true stories witnessed by a scientist who has lived among these Indians for decades. The illustrations are wonderful, too.

On Whales and Dolphins

Dolphin Man: Exploring the World of Dolphins, by Lawrence Pringle (New York: Atheneum, 1995).

The true story of a research scientist working to understand dolphins in the wild.

Looking at Dolphins and Porpoises, by Dorothy Hinshaw Patent (New York: Holiday House, 1989).

A zoologist writes about how dolphin babies grow up, how killer whales feed, and how scientists measure the intelligence of dolphins and porpoises.

Meeting Dolphins: My Adventures in the Sea, by Kathleen Dudzinski (Washington, D.C.: National Geographic Society, 2000).

Working with marine dolphins, the author studies their communication with the help of a listening device she invented.

Whales and Dolphins, by Anton Ericson (Chicago: Kidsbooks, 1994).

Learn how to tell male and female orcas apart, compare whale tails, and learn other interesting facts through great pictures and snappy text.

Rescue of the Stranded Whales, by Ken Mallory and Andrea Conley (New York: Simon and Schuster, 1989).

When three young pilot whales were stranded in Massachusetts in 1986, the New England Aquarium went to their rescue. This is the story of their long journey back to the wild ocean.

For Older Readers

Journey of the Pink Dolphins: An Amazon Quest, by Sy Montgomery (New York: Simon and Schuster, 2000).

This book describes in detail my four expeditions to the Amazon, where you can read more about Vera, Moises, and Gary and a host of other people and animals, too.

Index